THE LEGEND OF THE SINGING RAINBOW GUM TREE

BY

TARYN LANE KLANOT

ILLUSTRATED BY LIS SUNDBERG, JESSICA SUDOL, AND ASHLYNN RUTHERFORD

the PeppertreePress

Sarasota, Florida

ACKNOWLEDGEMENT

An enormous thank you to Julie Ann James and Teri Franco of
Peppertree Press for making my publishing dream a reality.

ISBN: 978-1-61493-572-8
Library of Congress Number: 2018900972
Printed February 2018

This book is dedicated
to my BELL and ESSYI families.

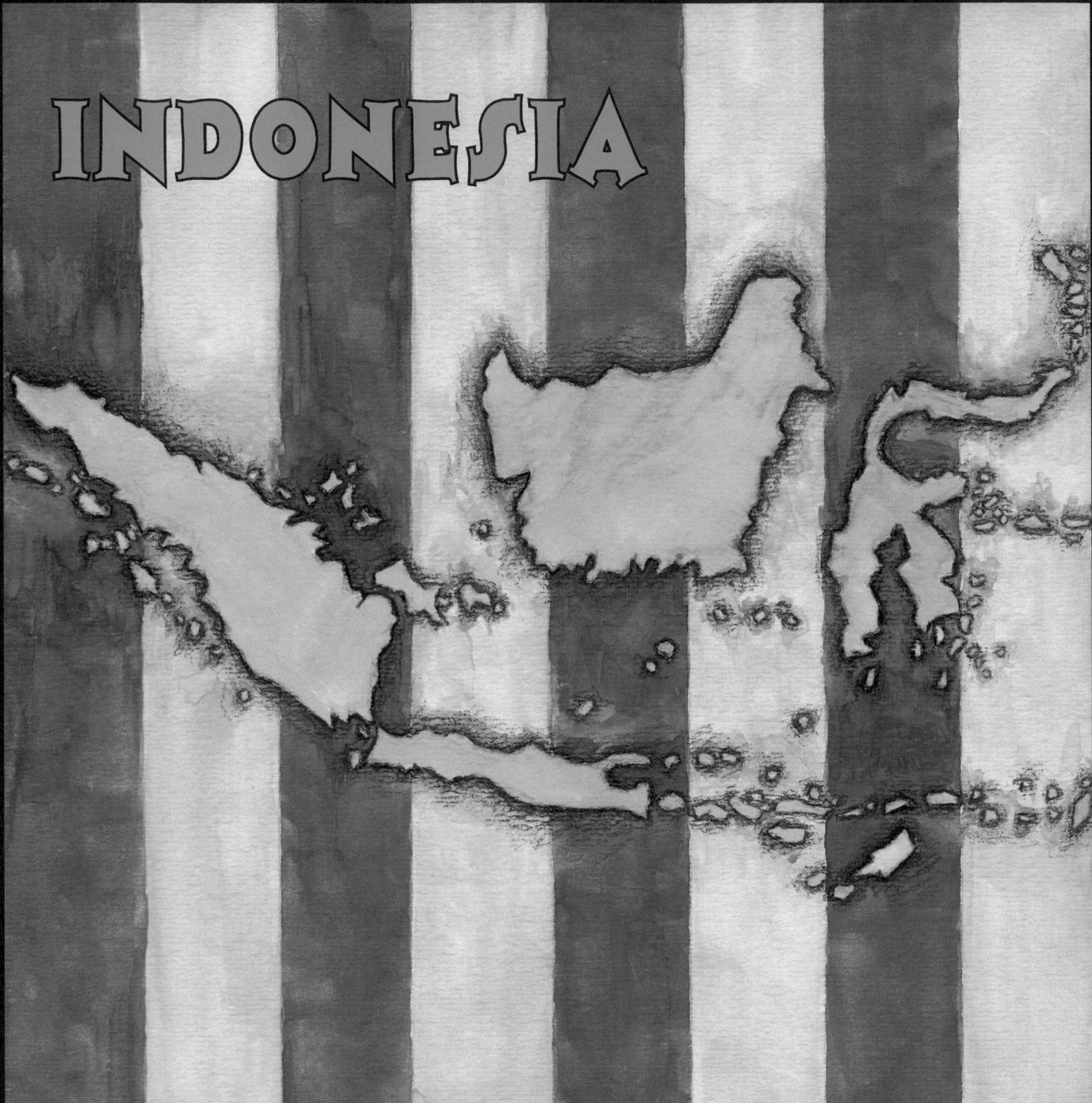
INDONESIA

There once was a tree who lived in a rainforest on the largest of the Indonesian Islands. She was a Rainbow Gum, named for the vibrant colors of her trunk. All of the animals loved her. She had the friendliest smile and her branches, like long limbs, gave the warmest of hugs. And, unlike all of the other Rainbow Gums on the island, this tree could sing.

Some grown-ups, the ones who cannot tell tree from shrub, will try to tell you that trees cannot sing, but they are wrong. I, myself, have heard the precious songs that the Rainbow Gum had to offer.

Her songs were sweeter than any sound an instrument could create. They were as powerful as a great waterfall, yet as gentle as a butterfly's touch. They were harmonious, heartfelt, and healing.

And with help from the waves and the winds, the tree's songs could be heard all over the world. But only those who listened carefully, and who kept an open-mind and an open-heart, could hear them.

Much like the sun, the tree spread warmth throughout the forest. And on sunny summer days, she would sing about mangos and miracles. The blissful Birds of Paradise would chirp along with her, and together they created a song powerful enough to bring light to anybody having a dark day.

And when the rains would come, the tree would sing a magical melody that would bring life to the forest. The raindrops seemed to dance along to the song, leaping from leaf to leaf. And below the canopy, the monkeys danced the mambo, the tigers danced the tango, and the bears danced the boogie-woogie.

And every evening, as the sun began to set, the tree would sing a soft, serene song that would bring the forest to a settle. Her song was like a lullaby. It was peaceful, and her words were calm and cool. The rhinos, the kangaroos, the komodo dragons, and all of the other forest friends gathered around the tree and prepared for sleep. The tree's song was so soothing that it would bring sleep upon even the spiniest of the spiny turtles and the sassiest of the sassy snakes in the forest.

Between the hours of dusk and dawn, as the elephants and the orangutans snored, and the crickets cried to the moon, the tree could be heard humming along.

It seemed as though the stunning songs would never end. The tree sang through every day and every night, through every season and every storm. Her marvelous music filled the heart of every listener.

But one woeful day, the tree stopped singing. Those who were used to hearing the tree's songs were heartbroken. The days that followed were silent and somber.

And then, something miraculous happened. The entire forest began to sing: every flower, every frog, every leopard, and every tree. They sang a single song, perhaps the sweetest song the world has heard. It was a song of hope.

It was at that miraculous moment when the rainforest, the one on the largest of the Indonesian Islands, earned its name: The Singing Forest.

It is not known for sure what happened to the singing Rainbow Gum on the day she stopped singing, but legend says that she was cut down. She was cut down by a company that cared only about their own success.

Her long, beautiful branches are thought to have been used for fuel for a fire, and her tall trunk thrown in the trash. The company used her space in the forest to grow a crop and to make a profit.

So, if you are ever lucky enough to hear a tree sing, whether it lives in your backyard or in The Singing Forest itself, go protect it. Make sure that nobody hurts it. Make sure that its sweet songs never die.

INFORMATION PAGE

Though the name is made up, The Singing Forest of Indonesia does exist, and all the animals present in this book can be found there. Of course, the precious Rainbow Gum Eucalyptus trees can also be found in Indonesia.

Indonesia is home to one of the world's largest areas of rainforest, and has one of the highest rates of deforestation.

The main cause of deforestation in Indonesia is the unsustainable production of palm oil. Roughly two and a half million acres of Indonesian rainforest is cleared each year, with intentions of using the cleared land to grow more palm oil.

No matter how near or far you are from The Singing Forest, you can help protect it! By buying products that contain sustainable palm oil, or no palm oil at all, you can prevent deforestation from occurring in Indonesia. You can also support this cause further by becoming more aware of the efforts of the many local and national organizations that are fighting deforestation.

100% of proceeds from the sale of this book will be donated to organizations fighting deforestation.

Photo References

https://www.nauwalenotours.com/natures-graffiti-eucalyptus-trees/

https://www.daleysfruit.com.au/forum/rainbow-eucalyptus/

http://pursue-news.com/2016/12/12/orangutans-palm-oil-progress/

https://www.ran.org/demand_the_palm_oil_front_runners_become_true_leaders

ABOUT THE AUTHOR:

Taryn Klanot (far left) is a student at Riverview High School in Sarasota, Florida. The inspiration to write this book came while studying environmental science at the Brown Environmental Leadership Lab and the Environmental Studies Summer Youth Institute. Taryn has always had a deep love for the environment and wishes to pursue a career in Environmental Studies.

ABOUT THE ILLUSTRATORS:

Lis Sundberg (middle left), Jessica Sudol (middle right), and Ashlynn Rutherford (far right) are IB Art students at Riverview High School in Sarasota, Florida. Lis is interested in Environmental Studies and is an active conservationist. Jessica is interested in art and business and has recently earned the Golf Key Scholastic Art and Writing Award. As well as a visual artist, Ashlynn is a pre-professional dancer and wildlife photographer.

CPSIA information can be obtained
at www.ICGtesting.com
Printed in the USA
LVIC06n2245280218
568228LV00001B/7

9 781614 935728